Fractured, Yet Healing

Fractured, Yet Healing

Grace in the Wilderness

ANDRA DURHAM

RESOURCE *Publications* · Eugene, Oregon

FRACTURED, YET HEALING
Grace in the Wilderness

Resource Publications
An Imprint of Wipf and Stock Publishers
199 W. 8th Ave., Suite 3
Eugene, OR 97401

www.wipfandstock.com

PAPERBACK ISBN: 978-1-6667-6373-7
HARDCOVER ISBN: 978-1-6667-6374-4
EBOOK ISBN: 978-1-6667-6375-1

VERSION NUMBER 031523

Grateful acknowledgement is made to the following for incorporation of Abba's word.

Scripture taken from the New King James Version®. Copyright © 1982 by Thomas Nelson. Used by permission. All rights reserved.

Eric,
Our Father
Loves you most.

Contents

Illustrations

Acknowledgments

Special acknowledgement is given to Mexico, she is a darling with breadth. Thank you friends for fortifying a home in my heart; home is everywhere.

fractured

Introductory Note

skeletonization

noun
skele·toniza·tion

1 : the befriending of detritus,
   wherein a lonely skeleton finds home.

Naked

Whispered love,
Murmured sighs.
Airy and breathless,
Sweet delights.

Stand before me
And reveal yourself to me:
The beauty and tragedy.

Remove the coins
Atop my eyes.
So, I may bask
In your view.

The Meditation

I sit in silence
And still
No meditation.

Chaos enraptures every thought.
It escalates, louder—
No meditation!

A sight to behold
Is the still man,
He meditates.

I silently observe
And pray in succession for your peace;
Meditate.

You breathe in and out
And harmonize with discordant sounds.
You meditate.

In awe of the stillness
I seek to ascertain;
He meditates.

Flat Earth

The image
We conceive
Of the world at—large
Collapses.

Tension rises
As our sun sets.

We forgot ourselves
And our passion dies
Like a smothered flame.

Once Removed

Morning light
Awakens a lazy
Reverie.

Effete movement
And existential crisise
Environ me.

Thoughts vie
To be released
Like smoke in lungs.

Stale air invites me
As grey thoughts
Charge to liberate
Our collective consciousness.

My freedom is taken
As I begin
To awaken.

Ennui

In a lust world
Eyes veil
Like the angel,
Apart.

Burnt orange days:
Hopscotch,
Purple Koolaid
And lace, ruffled socks.

The Black virgin,
Starry, *so* darling
With a grin as wide
As motioned double dutch—

Too soon taken and touched.

In a lust world
Eyes veil
Like the angel,
Apart.

Nada Mas

I wept,
"You broke my heart."
She laughed and chided:
"How many *times* can I break your heart?"

The Ganda proverb,
"One who loves you,
Warns you"
Races about
As I numb.

The frigid water
Is bitter
And warm.

Monster

In search of clarity,
He stands
Opposite to the mirror.

A monster reflects.

In his wake,
An atrophied heart
And calculated mind
Rage.

He is content
With his projected view.

A Dream Song: A Flower Deflowered

I ravished the honey in your garden.
Starved of delicacy so I overindulged.
Divorced intention;
I dreamt of you with green eyes in a red dress.
Masochistic proclivities
Ought harden.

The intensity of my arden,
You mirrored and divulged.
Contravention
And denial yields abstention.

O, garden.

There is no pardon:
Trauma frozen to that which culled.
For pain's indention,
The flowing of tears allays tension—
Not to be divulged.

A *garden*!

St. Patrick's Day

Donned in black,
Luck evaded me
As I was not prepared to receive.

His eyes were green
As shamrocks
And he drove snakes into
A once venerated *temple*.

His hands were black and overcast like
A most troubled ocean.

He moved the knight with tragic irony
And did not dare touch the bishop!

He spoke of his god,
A god whom allows his men to violate
And perverse his name.

This "god"
Demoralizes his beautiful brides.

Captured & Tortured

The knight's capture
Is our fall of grace.

The demon hath escaped
And like *hell* he seeks to wage war.

Nobility remains an army of one
And he is dualized.

To accept the place
Of a lesser man
Is his fall of grace.

A Falsehood

Cheap, plastic
Dream.

Your words failed
Without action's support.

Incepted by lies,
A troubled foundation
Collapses.

A godlike sight
Turns slight
And submits
To his shadow.

A projected sun
Blistered my mind
And calloused my skin.

I awaken alone.

Temporal

What value does intimacy hold
Among strangers?

The temporal connecting of flesh.
The exchange of frenzied thoughts
And feigned,
Priori understanding.

Herein this state,
One feels safe enough—
Within this *cheap* bubble of understanding
To release all doubt
And fear.

Do not fall prey
To the temptation of
Vulnerability.

The emotion associated with their touch
Will most assuredly fade,

That is—
Until you greet another
Dismal face.

Of Gods & Worms

O, genesis of man;
Our origination besought trials unknown.
The serpent posed
And we heeded and indulged.
Doth the forbidden fruit taste as sweet?
The Garden of Eden disfigured our souls!
Now men vie against their origination;
Noble is he that restrains and controls.

The jester's privilege:
Folly and freedom;
A scepter that mocks.
He mirrors that which he is not.
A sloth to self—imposed limitation
Like a bag of wind.
His protection does not supersede
The divine law for which he is pinned.

Matthew betold of debt's repayment,
Punishment for restoration,
"Ay me—
A vat of acid for purification?"
So you leapt from Mount Etna
Akin to your pies,
To the monarch's jovial surprise
All comical honesty dies.

Liminality of the mind,
Complacency of might
And authorship of life;
All neutrality is feigned.
Willful ignorance is an *opiate*!
Purgatorio has dawned
It is time
To abscond.

Of gods
And worms.

En Cuanto a Mí

Men journey
To conquer and disempower
The land and womb.

The siren's sympathetic
Magic
Lulls to violent men

Whispers of
Oceanic disappearances
Swim about
The pastel town.

She lays descansos for
Willful chicanery
And eagerness to misconstrue
Her song.

Their malevolence is swallowed
By the belly of the sea.

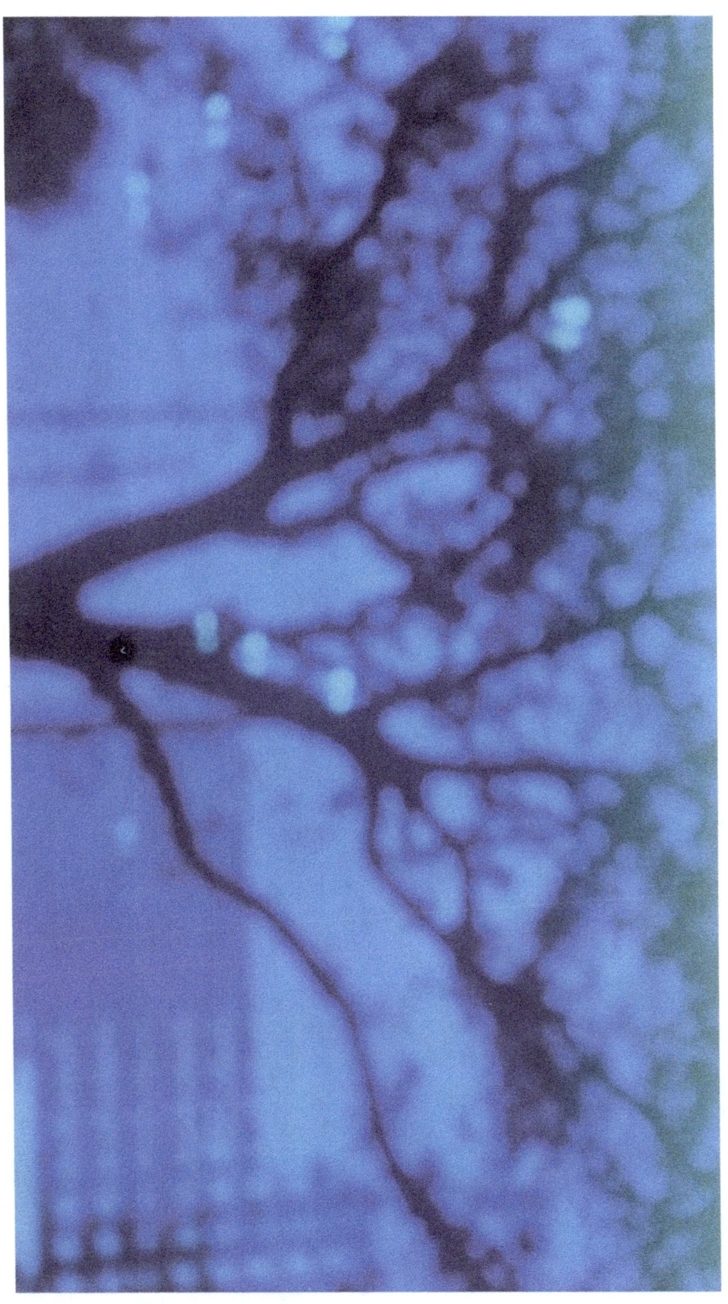

The Conquistador

The water
Solidified;
It is frozen.

"Tread lightly
Its depth
Remains uncharted."

He pillages despite
The maidens fair warning.

He dares to manipulate
With differentiated logic
And incept new life.

O, ye, anima
Which forgot
The sacrity of the womb!

528 Hz

Life bows
As fight precedes.

Awoken from a slumber,
Flowers rise
From concrete;
A shrine to behold.

Outside of the cave,
He reaches for
The sun.

Withered and weary
But
He is young.

Colossal thoughts
Search
For the light
Of the sun.

healing

Introductory Note

positive—phototropism

noun
pos·i·tive— pho·tot·ro·pism

1 : growth towards love.

The Divine Feminine

It is spring.

On the *Court of Women,*
We dance
And express gratitude
For wisdom and life
Donned in white.

We reflect upon
The hands of Mars
That touched and marred
The exterior
Of our silver temple,
Erected for Venus.

We must purify the inside
To prevent the vulgar
Reach of their hands
From corrupting *us*
Within.

Tapestry's depict chaos in motion.
In modest lighting,
Timeless art captures.
The Acacias mirror
Our feminine luster
And divine protection.

We harmonize
With the sounds of heaven
And cleanse one another
In the Siwa Oasis.

We are protected
Even when taken
By the touch of man.

Raison d'Être

My Father adjures obedience.
Man requires clear permission to act
With immaculate, soulless expedience;
Obedience to abstract and exact.

Abstain from darkening the canvas' white
Abstain from tormenting the unblemished;
Discipline's teeth do not bite.
The machined, disheartened mind *is* blemished!

To still with all that is holy, settled,
Contrasts against the droned onning of man.
O, to be adorned in *heaven*, petaled,
Chatters the sad boast of the man who ran.

Father's honor grants a reason to be.
Father's honor grants a reason to be.

Daisy Reflections

Delights
Of Soul enclose
The angels whisperings.
I hear the harp with feathered strings.
I see
Thy stark Heaven of the Fixed Stars.
I eat from Your garden,
It doth satiate.
Selah.

The Lady

An Angelica blooms,
It is as unexpected as it is beautiful.

An Aster dies.
A willow blooms.

The grace of age
Surrounds the sage.

An Iris blooms,
It is as unexpected as it is beautiful.

Sabanas

Sabanas,
A twist in the sheets?

Innocence—
Stark and white.

Purity that parallels
Those unsullied,
White sheets.

Ragnarok

Crushed flowers,
Droop despair
And pool sorrow's rot.

Persephone's screams
Impregnate
Baubo's belly
And silence.

The old, laden
Sun
Curtseys its set.

Demeter's shadow,
Fertility to:

"Die! Die! Die!"

A crux'd twilight
Wars
And laughs.

Far—stretched, rosy flowers
Extend to face the daughter'd sun.

Loss is absent.

The Empress Card

the weight of the crown
reinforces a brevity
unbeknownst to most

gracious in all states
despite the stones they will cast
it turns to gold in her hands

stoic and maternal
she tempers inferno
and tends to her garden

The Moon is Fixed

Does brilliance remain luminous and pure?
The men oar against the calm of our tide,
And vex balance like disturbance to a wave.
Despite souls cycling; a moon to endure.
Dying and transitive yet humans stride.
The moon's known gaze continues to outbrave.
A great solace is to be unperturbed
Like the processional of a bride.
Does the soul recall bearing fruits to crave?
Please enliven your gaze for the despaired,
To save.

Thrice I Saw

Reactions the archer restrains
To avert the release of triviality
And a failed target.

In a dream,
The archer appeared to me.
She armed me with
Bow and arrow.

Desire roves
And craves
Outside the soul.

Child,
The world is inside of your soul.
Pray to hearken thy ears.

The devil distracts
With dimmed lights
And vice.

Pray to hearken thy ears,
Focus
And release.

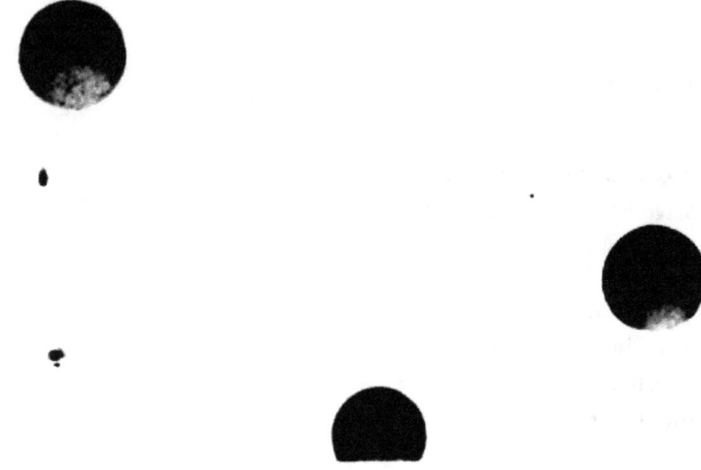

Island

An island,
I land on Self.
Solitude provided by God himself.

Grown into you—
Alone,
But never blue.
Stillness is tried and true.
I yearn for a book from the shelf.

No man can entreat.
Sorrow is now obsolete!

Serenity is sweet.

Alas, truest to myself.

By My Own Hands

Displacement begets the desire to ground
As the storm wails to be soothed and cooed.

Judgment seeks strength.

Can misanthropic somber
Escape the fun house's
Distorted view?

Claustrophobia:
Ceaseless noise.

I part and stand upright alone.

Facing myself in the mirror,
I cut my hair,
Again.

Aloneness

No one hears as much as silence.

No one strengthens as much as those who have
Passed and surrendered
Their swords.

Guarded and comforted by my angels;
I am never alone!

Loneliness
Desynchronizes man
From his brother.

The grayed man too understands;
We sit apart
And exclaim loudly
In silence.

La Que Sabe

Her seraphs guide
Against slow, moving tides
To holy North!

She trumpets
A lunar laugh
To expose the rats of night.

Father illuminates her path:

A daylight frenzy ensues
And eclipses
The beasts and cadgers alike.

—

Zion twinkles in her eyes.

Psychomachia

The Ivorian Djed Pillars
Of Your daughters
Upright.

Alpha and Omega,
Wisdom to war:

Harrows of womanhood.

A bird song,
A blinding
And Oedipal disgrace
Confuse Your natural law.

Lot *is* grieved.

Daughters to salt,
Wombs to dust!

Common objects,
Aimlessly drift
As defiling hands
In the cities of the plain.

Alpha and Omega,
Wisdom and war:

Sulfur and fire.

Ezekiel,
Our daughters slumber to harps
Not to be roused
Awaken her to hope.

"Protect her as a lamb without blemish."[1]

1. Ezek 46:13 NKJV.

Grandmother's Dirge

You foretold of
Fast girls
And soulless temptations.

You imparted both
Dearness and spice
As honey is not palatable alone.

To sew with you once more
Would weave
My years in gold.

Hair like Hekla's peak
And eyes still
With the sea.

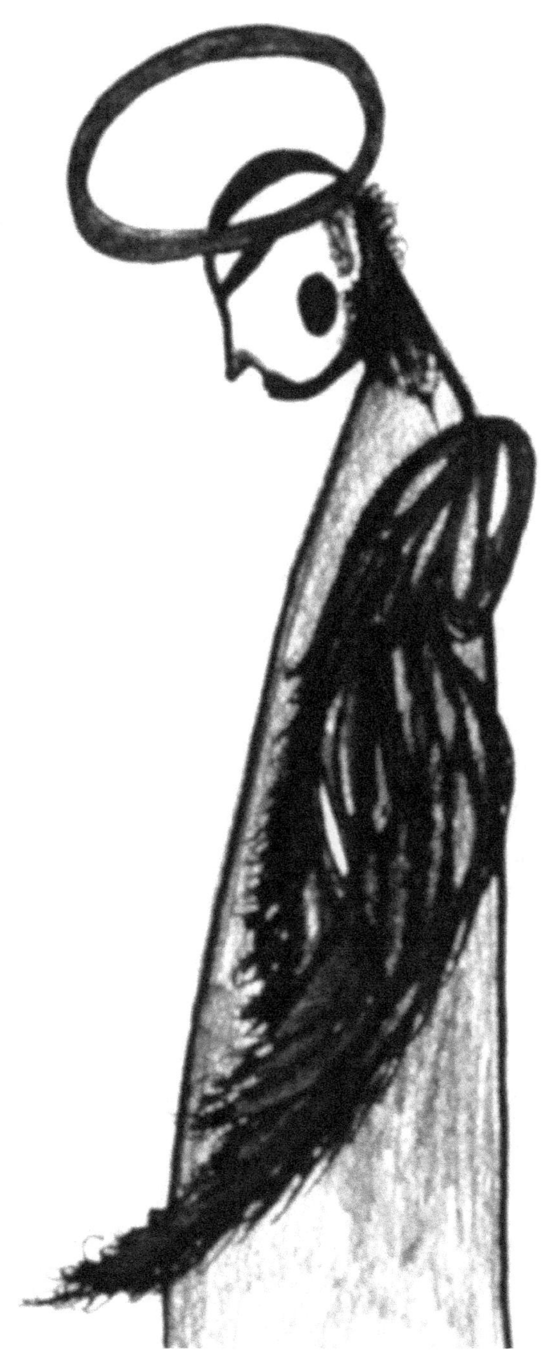

Trust Fall

I.

Father,

I rest my head upon Your palm.

It is a relief to focus on that which is within my control, and not the calamity of the world nor the equilibrium of the stars.

I could never be a "god" as your shield is my sole source of strength.

Obedience to You
Dissolves ego
And absolves my heart.

Instead of selfish vainglory;
I surrender to You.

Trust Fall

II.

Tomorrow is not promised
And I no longer forsake the day
Nor make a victim of tomorrow.

To slumber with idleness
Is to indulge in restless sleep.

To feast
Without hunger
Is to fatten
The ox.

To avert from
Your promise
Is to die
Without the hope
Of light.

Eudaemonia

The lilies in the garden
Reminisce
Of youth.

A pure,
Unadulterated sight.

The breeze
Tickles my soul
And animates my skin.

Virtuosity
Is timeless
And grace transcends.

The present
Remains breathtakingly simple
In its elegance.

Innocent and fulfilled
Amidst the lilies
In the garden.

Uptown Girls

Child debauched
The richness of chocolate.
Now,
Parent offers hunger
To know balance.

A cheeky face
Forgot to
Somber
And chisels
His epitaph
Till the grave.

There remains a
Time and place.

Maturation knows restraint.

Daylight (For the Discouraged)

The world awaits you;
Dare to hope!

The oyster's defense
Is its pearl.

So then,
Beauty guards.

As bad company
Corrupts good morals,
So too,
Cynicism maligns faith.

Our antidote is
Action contrary
To our source of pain.

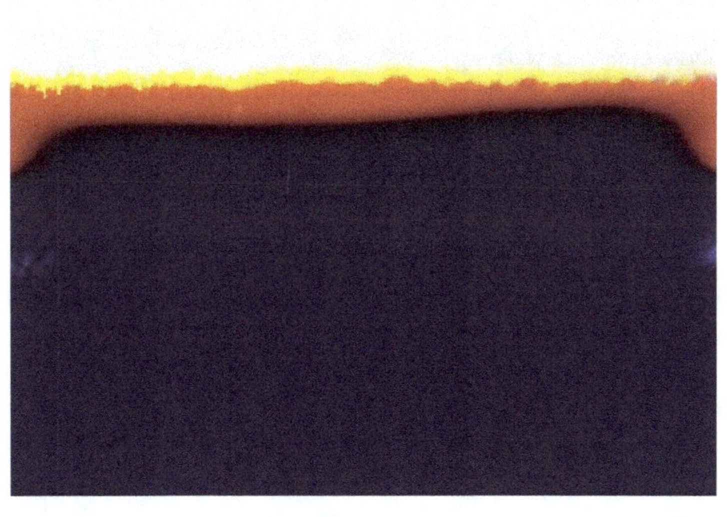

On Pain

Pain demands
To be acknowledged
As a festering wound
Deserves air.

At first,
I identified malaise
As a threat.

Its pain angered my folly
And from its grasp,
I had to escape.

Discomfort is a warning
Alarmed by
The spirit.

Yes,
It hurts.

No,
We will not forget.

The denial of pain
Stalemates
The possibility of joy.

I cry,
As I write;

The
Poppies,
Daises
And orchids
Reward me with growth.

Obedience

They disappear like smoke:
Yesterday's dismay
Illuminates the mire to cleanse today.
Helplessness to revoke
So they disappear like smoke.

Decisiveness weighs, no morals sway
Farewell to child's play.
I will not pass under the yoke;
They disappear like smoke.

Fruits to repay,
Purpose to obey
Conviction to invoke.
They disappear like smoke.

(A Lament) Yo Trato

O, Solomon:
Please sharpen my sword.

O, Blessed Virgin Mary:
The men make women dry,
And vanquishing purity is the talk of the time.

O, Basquiat:
Why did they not see you in time?

At equilibrium
The sun and moon
Sustain the tide.

Once we were *pure* crystalline!

Grandfather time presents
The choice to refine.

Wisdom gently frees
The noose of vice.

Deliverance

A Frankensteinian abstraction,
Stranger in Satan's home.
Incepted in hatred and faction.
Angst encouraged me to roam.
In bathtubs, I lie down—
No antidote to down
To erase the evil; to repose.
Cold blankets to enclose:
Does lukewarmth garner praise?
Morrow shocked as sorrow rose.
A ghost to love's sweet gaze.

Orion's light provided satisfaction
Despite tears that could fill an astrodome.
Ought regarded as a fraction,
A louse on a silver comb.
Sorrow wore the crown
And joy was an asinine clown.
To the stars I offered logos,
A spirit to presuppose.
Adrift in the Yangtze,
Naked in a sandstorm, praying as I expose.
Alone in a great maze.

I busied myself with distraction;
A stranger to my home.
Numb to reaction
Though rage convulsed with foam.
Smiles masked a despaired frown
As I escaped downtown.
Vice indulged, fractures and slows;
Spirit sprinted to dispose.
Drowning and ablaze,
He asked if my misery peaked like meadows?
Shocked to be object to a *loving* gaze.

Virgin Suicides

To observe
Hopelessness in youth
Is to bear
Nonsensical despair.

The earth is on fire
And we seek Heaven's tranquility.

Heartbeats stop—

Once the world ceases to listen.

Ego furthers shame
And noise
Abets silence.

Have we neglected that
Redemption is timeless?

On Heavenward Devotion

Manifold experience
Disciplined in Thy mercy,
Softens the edge of a whetted past;
Aright on thy geodesic path.

Beautified with golden Kintsugi
To illuminate
Thy transformative repair.

Clay to thy will
Gherian architecture
To Thy mold.

Opportunity

Ahead of
The Magi
Went the star.

Gold for the rising of our King,
Frankincense for liminal days
And myrrh to fortify the dusk.

O, ye,
Children of the Lamb,
Paled *yet* mirrored innocence
Shepherded
To expand,
A lament for thy woes.

Contrition for awareness of this perpetual,
Undying *stain*
Yields to fight:
A blunted sword
To a musket;
A maggot to a king.

We enlighten for
The brightness of *Your* dawn.

This Woman's Utterance

The sorrowful way
For impermeable,
Profaned dust?
O, gravel to heart!
We corrupt the waters of the ocean,
Ration as pigs,
Deny peace
And brotherhood;

Yet you present *us* a gift.

Of bastard Judas,
Agency,
The soul
And divine will.

Weary yet I know not *a* travail
Hands graciously tremor
To accept
And embody Your gift.

Tropic of Cancer

Imaginary spheres,
Veiled, heavenly bodies
So it is *observed*.

Be not afraid of the sun.
Do not eschew its light.

Though the sun
Drifts southward
In June
Its grandeur remains.

The ecliptic is traversed
And his favor is
Centered upon us.

Miller demanded
Everything or nothing—
Thoughts adjacent to the sun!

To quietly appreciate
The passage of seasons
Apart from
The pride of lions
Is to return.

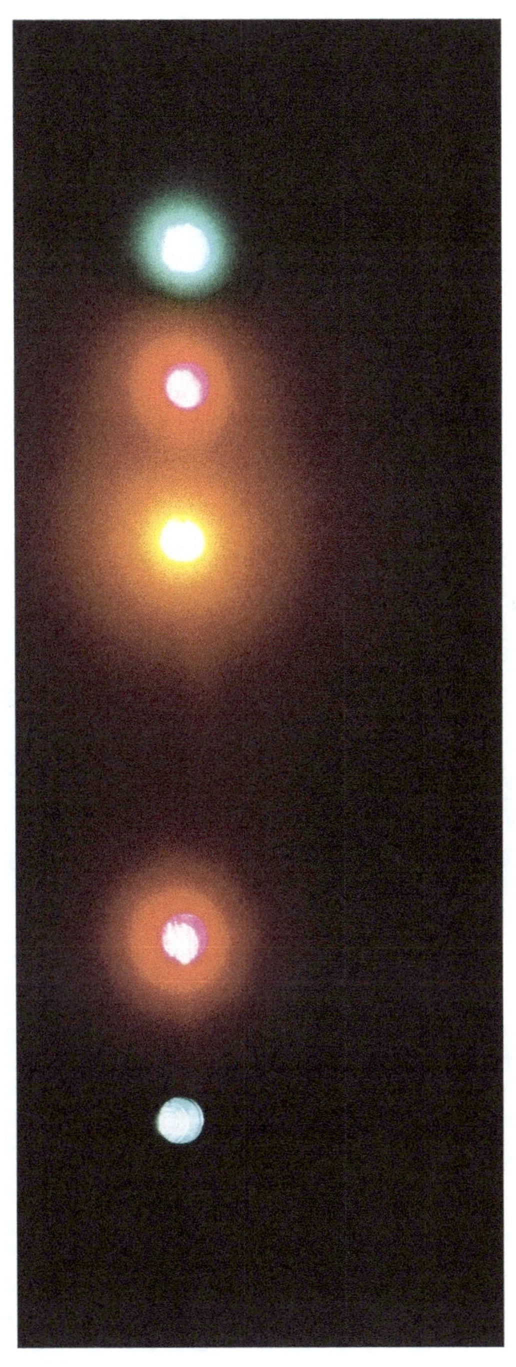

XXIII

The enchanting lands suffer and dry.
Wisdom bodes us time.
Lord, usher a wind to sound the chime.
Hearest not her cry?
The power of Versailles
Is as futile as burnt offerings and thyme.
We spring in summertime
For it is You to whom we rely.
The old field of wildflowers
Do not doubt.
The sun rises in Your hours.
Loyalty's supplication ascends about.
The earth showers
And You assuage *every* doubt.

Fuchsia

Animate us to life!

Summon your hummingbirds:
To avert us from
Wound scarlet secrets,
Spiraling upwards
Those mahogany stairs
Sans the tock of time.

Nourish us,
Your court
With royal hymns,
The wisdom of the tiger
And grandiosity of Kabuki.

Water our souls
With the very water
From which you
Grow.

Embolden us
As a geisha amid shadows,
A peacock in a sepia desert.

Strike in us
Courage!

Dye our souls in your hue.

Nesting

I spin my cocoon in silk and slowly digest myself.

On Water

Baptismal ceremonies I do not recall.
Bare and small;
Burdened, the water speaks to me.
Buoyant rain against my flesh:
Bovine renewed as a dove.
Bravado kneels to
Brevity of flesh affirming the
Burgeoning of Soul.

Un Nueva Dia

Palliative efforts inspire hope,
Ubiquitous aims cast deadly stones to Soul.
Rationalization alone deprives art of *its* science.
Pacifism is key to reaction's giant.
Obsolete maxims
Sequesters those who heed its wisdom.
Encumber ego's frivolity.

Implore of yourself and
Stray from sycophants.

Kinetic objects
Elucidate this wisdom.
Yonder is morrow.

Sweet Tea & Cigarettes

Christopher became a name
Synonymous with Michael,
Uriel and Gabriel.

A neighbor that
Never asked to be father
Yet brotherly
And paternal kept
Me safe under his wing.

He reminded me
That God too
Calls me by name.

Purity
And unconditional love
Rescued me.

I welcome the day
To celebrate in Heaven
With chosen kin.

42 Days

Cemented
And dysrhythmed
Steps

Level.

The monarch's
Epitethed message,

Flutters
And spans

Etheric hues

Of blushed secrets
And a befriended youth.

Santa Julia

On a scroll that spans the earth,
Pregnant thoughts
Spill
Indiscriminate
And pure
As a robbed monk
Onlooking.

Non—attachment surrenders me
As the release
Of a pink ballon.

To catch and release
Stars
Delimbs and disjoints
The constellation.

Orion's strength
Beseeches me
To receive;
Raphael nurtures me
To give.

Forecast: Eternal Sunshine with Bouts of Rain

Long—suffering imparts patience.
Wisdom ascertained is experience lived
Your luster for life darkened complacence.

Patient optimism sparked a renascence,
As you understand there is no unbearable pain.
Pay due obeisance

To your nascence
And never complain.
Time quells impatience.

A Year Ago

At night,
Apartment lights turn red.

She gutturally cries,
Bled and bred.

My orchid turns the deepest blue
Like Coltrane's schismic morning dread.

Water and fire awaken the dead.

My purity races ahead
To protect the sisters unsaid:
Soulless and bound by a bedspread.

South Korea

Rash and provocative
Strikes
Will not intimidate
The boldness
Of the red pine
Nor defang our tiger:

"It is not for kings."[2]

Elegant,
Scattered melodies
And silk strings
Zither to strength.

Willpower ought conquer the craven.

2.. Prov 31:4 NKJV.

I Have Limits

Touch is to heal not harm;
My body demands honor.
I despise winks, bluffed charm
And leeches with a biting proclivity to fawner.

Love does not disarm
And disrespect will be informed
As my foundation is rooted and formed.
Against evil my sword is drawn,
And virtue is my defense to brawn.
Solace hath transformed.

Cloudless

Hope
Grows to believe.

Father, I Ask to be Tall

O, Father, please
Quiet the desire to control.
Brute force to ease,
Weightless as leaves moved by Your breeze.
Fractures to renew as whole,
Exposure that receives atoll;
Prayer for reprise.

Maundy Thursday

Born for adversity
O, to cleanse thy second heart;
A sweet Govindan part.

The prodigal son,
Quixotic and brick
Wise to repent.

Locusts
And wild honey
Primes the gong of Soul.

Mirrors:
Eyes and union
An incidental reflection.

A vernal equinox,
Sweet diptych
Of Self.

A Revelation

Terrene
Blood and breath
Torpids,

Too,

"The kingdoms of the world and their splendor."[3]

Eternal water
Cascades
To restore thy soul.

Anchor not to
Prodigalic treasures
Laden upon the androgynous ocean floor.

Compass
To Abba:

Kindled fire in a black winter,
Symphonic wind for the battement of leaves,
A harp amid despaired silence,
And key holder to thy soul.

O, precious star!

3. Matt 4:8 NKJV.